IMAGES
of America

NAUGATUCK

View looking north on Church Street. This photograph was taken from the post office, then located in the Barnum Building at the left. The many-windowed building on the right is the "coat shop" where rubber raincoats were made. At this time roads were not paved.

Cover Image: The Goodyear Metallic Rubber Shoe Co. and staff on Rubber Avenue.

IMAGES
of America

NAUGATUCK

Dana J. Blackwell
and the Naugatuck Historical Society

ARCADIA

First published 1996
Copyright © Dana J. Blackwell, 1996

ISBN 0-7524-0415-6

Published by Arcadia Publishing,
an imprint of the Chalford Publishing Corporation
One Washington Center, Dover, New Hampshire 03820
Printed in Great Britain

Library of Congress Cataloging-in-Publication Data applied for

View from the lawn of the Congregational church looking southeast. One can see the new Naugatuck Savings Bank of 1910, the Whittemore Memorial Library of 1894, the Naugatuck National Bank of 1893, and the old Naugatuck Town Hall of 1882.

Contents

Beautiful new station. The relocation of the railroad tracks in 1906 and 1907 necessitated the construction of a new station. Mr. J. H. Whittemore agreed to pay for the building in part if he could choose the architect. Henry Bacon, famed architect of the Lincoln Memorial in Washington, was chosen and he produced a remarkably handsome building which was completed in 1910.

Introduction

The towns of the Naugatuck River Valley have much in common. Their hilly terrain and glacial soil precluded any great success at farming with the result that, very early, they turned their attention to crafts that could make use of available water power from plentiful brooks. When the Industrial Revolution began to influence New England, many communities were ready to embrace new concepts in manufacturing. Much of the Naugatuck River area was affected by these new ideas. However, in spite of similar trends throughout the area, each community had some unique features, usually the result of individual citizens with special qualities and interests. By the mid-nineteenth century, Naugatuck was called the "rubber town." Had it not been for Charles Goodyear's growing up here, this would not have happened. If a few families in Waterbury had not taken an early interest in metal production and processing, Waterbury would not have become the "brass city."

Though many features of Naugatuck's history have been swept away by time, the invention of photography in 1839 made possible the preservation of images of people and scenes that were part of everyday life. This book offers a selection of photographs from the Naugatuck Historical Society, plus some loaned by individuals from their private collections, to give residents of today an idea of how the town looked in former times. It is felt this is timely because so many things of the past have been destroyed through "progress" that many people now have no idea how things once looked. The illustrations contained within provide Naugatuck scenes and events up to about 1960.

This compilation has been the result of the efforts of many people, particularly the committee that has had numerous meetings and spent many hours studying available material and selecting photographs to be used. The committee was composed of the following members: Howard Burke, chairman; Dana Blackwell; Verna Blackwell; Sandra Clark; David Ebersole; William Ford; and Robert Stauffer.

Special recognition and thanks are owed to Howard Burke, chairman of the photo committee, who gave a great amount of time to having photos copied, doing extensive layout work, organizing the photographs, and working with the publisher.

Special thanks also to Robert Stauffer, Stella Pocoski, and Herminda Scally for their efforts on the chapter entitled Sports Heroes. Their work gathering pictures, identifying individuals, and furnishing information on outstanding teams is greatly appreciated.

View of Church Street looking north from the Maple Street intersection. Included in this 1915 image are: (right) the old town hall, the National Bank, the Savings Bank, several houses, and the post office; (left) the Congregational church, several houses, the dome of the St. Francis School, and the spire of the St. Francis Church. The grass borders between the road and the sidewalk with their arching trees were later removed to widen the road for automobile traffic.

One
School Days

From its earliest days, Naugatuck (Salem Society) was very interested in the education of its citizens. In 1730, while still a part of Waterbury, it established a school district. Salem Society was founded as an ecclesiastical organization in 1773, and for many years the group managed the schools which later operated with as many as eight independently run districts.

In 1852, several districts were consolidated to form the Union District. A new schoolhouse was constructed for the Union District on the Green across from the present Salem School. The upper floor was used as the high school and the lower floor as a primary school. This building served the town until 1894, when Salem School was completed.

Naugatuck's early schools were usually one-room, single-floor wood buildings, except for the Straitsville District school, which was a two-story building erected in 1825 and used until early in this century. Later, the Whittemore family gave the town three fine masonry schools which were considered, when built, among the finest in the country. Salem, the oldest school, built in 1894, is still serving the community.

Center District School, in use from 1811 to 1849. This one-room, ungraded school served what was then Judd's Meadow. This building was originally on the east side of town but was moved just north of Pine Hill Cemetery to replace a school built there in 1773.

Pond Hill School, built in 1822. This building was used until it was replaced with a new building in 1906. It was later sold and converted to a home.

An 1823 schoolhouse. This schoolhouse was erected on what is now Scott Street to serve the needs of the Lewistown District, formed in 1779. It was in use until 1852, when the larger Union District School was built on the Green opposite the present Salem School.

Straitsville School on New Haven Road, built about 1825. This was a graded school in a two-story building, unusual at a time when other town schools were one-story, one-room schools. It was used into the early decades of this century.

Middle District School. The Middle District, in the southern section of town, was established in 1778. This building was built in 1852 and was used until early in this century.

Union District (Consolidated) School, built in 1852. This structure contained Naugatuck's first high school, located on the second floor. The section on the right was part of the old St. Michael's Episcopal Church, purchased by the town and moved to the north side to provide additional space for the growing school population in 1876. It was used until 1894.

East Side Union City School, built on Prospect Street in 1872. After Hop Brook School was built, this building was sold and became a residence.

West Side Union City School on School Street. Built about 1876, this school was heated by stoves and had no inside plumbing, but remained in use until 1916. After Hop Brook School was built, it was used as a tenement house for a while before demolition.

Rubber Avenue, built in 1888. This grammar school served the south central part of town.

Oak Street School. This grammar school with lower grades was built to serve a portion of the east side of town. It is shown in this photograph as it appeared about 1900.

Millville School. The Millville District was established when the South West District was dissolved in 1836. It first had the usual one-room school but later, this larger, two-story building was built. When the Millville District was abolished, this building was sold and remodeled into a residence that bore no resemblance at all to this structure.

Salem School, designed by Mckim, Mead and White of New York. Completed and occupied in 1894, this building was a gift to the town from Mr. J. H. Whittemore. It was the first masonry school in town and served as a high school in the upper portion and a grammar school below. It had a modern heating and ventilating system (for the time) and electric lighting.

Central Avenue School. This handsome and attractive building was erected in the 1890s.

Prospect Street School. Union City's educational facilities were greatly improved in 1898 with the building of this school. It was one of Naugatuck's more attractive wooden educational facilities, with architectural character and commodious classrooms, but was demolished in 1957 to make way for the present school.

Groveside School. This school served children in the southern portion of town along New Haven Road and was used in the early decades of this century. It had only four grades.

Beebe Street School. This grammar school provided for the lower grades in the west-central portion of town and served Naugatuck through 1946. It stood vacant for a few years and was then demolished about 1950.

St. Francis Parochial School, completed in 1900. St. Francis School contained, at that time, one of the largest halls in the borough.

New Pond Hill School, erected in 1906. It was later sold for residential use.

Naugatuck High School. A gift of Mr. J.H. Whittemore, this building was designed by McKim, Mead and White. It was completed in 1904 and was equipped with a gymnasium and an indoor track, and had chemistry and physics laboratories. There were three floors with a street entrance on each. The building was equipped with splendid classical statuary, and contained pictures of world-renowned buildings and writers.

St. Hedwig's School. This school was established on the first floor of the church on Golden Hill Street, a few years after the wood-frame building was completed in 1910.

Hop Brook School. A gift from Harris Whittemore Sr., this school was built in 1916 to serve Union City children and to replace the two old wooden Union City schools. Theodate Pope Riddle, America's first distinguished woman architect, designed it. A recent addition (1994) has nearly doubled its size but maintained its remarkable architectural character.

Drawing room in the former high school (now Hillside).

Sewing room in the former high school. This interior shot was taken when the building was new.

Machine shop in the former high school.

Students in Grade 6A at Salem School, 1914. This class consisted of fifty pupils, as did most classes in those days.

Two
Early Churches

The church has been the spiritual and social center of community life in New England since the first Europeans settled here. Because of the early settlers' Puritan backgrounds, the town church was usually Congregational, but later, settlers of Anglican persuasion came to the region. In 1782, Naugatuck's first church building was built on the east side of town so that people would not have to travel to Waterbury, especially during the winter. Later the Episcopalians (Anglicans) built a small church in Gunntown. This building was later taken down and moved to the Green in 1832, and it served the parish until the present brick Gothic church was completed in 1876. In the 1840s, seeking to escape the potato famine in Ireland, a number of Irish immigrants settled in Naugatuck. By 1866 a Roman Catholic parish was established using a small wooden church on Water Street. Later, as the parish grew, it was superseded by the St. Francis Church on Church Street, which looks much the same today as it did when it was built (1882–90).

Later churches of denominations to serve Swedish, German, Polish, and other national groups were built. Today, the town has many handsome church structures of varied styles scattered throughout. The towers of these places of worship add greatly to the skyline, but more importantly, these institutions enrich the town through the transmission of strong values which build character and citizenship.

Congregational church. The Congregational Ecclesiastical Society was established in May 1773. The church was organized on February 22, 1781, as the "Congregational Church of Salem." The first church building, built in 1782, stood on a hill on the east side of town until 1831, when it was moved to the Green. In 1853 it was sold and moved to the east side of Church Street, where it became the Spencer store. This view shows it after it was moved from the Green to Church Street where the southern portion of the Neary Building now stands.

St. Michael's Episcopal Church. Early Episcopalians in Naugatuck attended church in Waterbury, but in 1786 they established their own society and met in homes until 1803, when a simple church structure was raised in Gunntown. It was removed and set up on the Green in 1832. It served until the present Gothic structure was built in 1876.

Methodist church. The first Methodists in Naugatuck met in homes in the 1820s and later in Pond Hill School. They built a church on Water Street in 1851 which was later moved to Church and Maple Streets in 1868. When a new church was built on Meadow Street, this was sold in 1886 and became a clothing store. This building was demolished to make way for the Neary Building.

Second Congregational church building. Built on the site of the early church on the Green in 1853–54, this church was used until June 15, 1902. The classic spire was very high and could be seen from a great distance.

St. Francis Roman Catholic Church (originally called St. Anne's). Built on Water Street, this structure was first used in 1857. The name was changed to St. Francis and the church was made a regular parish in 1866.

Present St. Michael's Church, completed in 1876. The building was made of brick with stone dressings, a fancy multicolored slate roof, and a partially free-standing tower. It has served the parish well for over 120 years.

Methodist church on Meadow Street. The church is shown here shortly after it was built in 1886.

Salem Lutheran Church. This church was established by a group of Swedish immigrants and erected on Salem Street in 1888. The parsonage was built south of it at about the same time. Transepts were later added to the church, and some years afterwards a brick addition was constructed on the east side.

St. Francis Church. The George Hine property on Church Street was purchased in 1877. Ground was broken here on April 7, 1882, for the present St. Francis Church. The basement was completed in 1883 and served until the church was finished on November 30, 1890. James Murphy of Providence, Rhode Island, was the architect and the cost of the structure was $19,000. The inspiration for the building was St. Gertrude's in Louvain, Belgium. A new rectory was completed in 1903.

Hillside Covenant Church. Organized in 1894 by a group of Swedish immigrants, this was originally called Swedish Bethany Congregational Church, but it was later renamed Hillside Congregational Church. The church was erected in 1899 and later remodeled into colonial style with a central spire. Pews from the old Congregational church on the Green were acquired when that church was demolished and have been used ever since.

The Congregational church. After demolition of the church on the Green, the present church, designed by McKim, Mead and White, was dedicated on May 20, 1903.

Immanuel Lutheran Church. A group of citizens of German background decided to build this church around 1900. It was dedicated in 1903, and in 1972 it was extensively remodeled to its present form. The church's location is striking because of its position high on a hill.

St. Paul's Lutheran (Lithuanian) Church. Built on Curtis Street in 1907, this church was destroyed in the flood of 1955. It was replaced with a new church on Millville Avenue.

St. Hedwig's Roman Catholic Church. The first Polish family came here in 1886 and other families followed. St. Hedwig's was organized by ninety-five Polish families in 1906. For services, they met in Sokolowski's Hall, but they built this church in 1910, which remained in use until a new church was erected in 1968.

St. Mary's Roman Catholic Church. This church was built for the expanding Roman Catholic population on the east side of Naugatuck. The Gothic structure and its two towers were designed and partially completed by Michael Donahue of Hartford. Lewis Walsh of Waterbury completed its construction in 1923. The c. 1855 John Isbell house was used as a rectory until a new brick one was built in 1938.

The 1886 Methodist Church on Meadow Street as it looked after it was later remodeled in colonial style.

Holy Savior Church. The congregation of the Holy Savior (Polish National Catholic) Church, organized about 1924, built this building on North Main Street about 1930. In 1955 it was swept away by the flood, leaving only the stairs and part of the foundation. In 1958, a fine new church was built on higher ground on Prospect Street.

Three
Important Buildings

Naugatuck began as a farming community in the early 1700s, but the hilly terrain and rocky glacial soil made farming difficult, and quite early led people to utilize the brooks for water power to run small shops. In the nineteenth century, the effects of the Industrial Revolution in Britain brought about the factory system, and for the first time, machinery was used to mass produce goods. This brought dramatic changes to New England towns, making home crafts all but obsolete. More and more people worked in factories. These workers were often paid minimal wages but the factory owners enjoyed the fruits of profitable manufacturing. Industrialists not only built themselves substantial residences but often put up buildings such as schools, churches, office blocks, libraries, and other structures to improve the appearance of the town where they lived.

Naugatuck was endowed with some fine buildings as a result of industrial success. Mr. J.H. Whittemore is particularly remembered for the first masonry and architecturally important schools, the public library, and other structures. The following photographs show buildings, some still standing and others gone, that were considered landmarks through the years.

Beecher Inn on Church Street. The Litchfield Turnpike tollhouse is on the right. The nearby dam was built in 1824 to provide water power to the shops on Water Street. In 1832, Daniel Beecher deeded the Green to two church congregations that soon built structures there.

Naugatuck Hotel. Once used as the town hall, this building was located on the east side of South Main Street, on the corner of Maple. It was removed to make way for the new Route 8.

Collins Hotel in Straitsville, built in 1811. This was a famous stopping place for stages on the Litchfield Turnpike between Litchfield and New Haven. It was demolished in September 1975.

Nichols Block on South Main Street, built in the 1850s. The third floor was a large hall used for graduations, theater productions, high school exhibitions, and other such activities. It was destroyed by the flood of 1955 when the west wall collapsed into the river.

Hotchkiss Block. Housing the post office, this block was on the east side of Water Street. It was torn down along with several other buildings to build the railroad tracks along the west side of the river.

Office of A.J. Pickett of the Tuttle Hoe Shop. A.J. Pickett served as first treasurer of the Naugatuck Savings Bank and carried on the bank's business here from 1870 to 1873.

Commercial Hotel. This is a good view of the hotel on the west side of Main Street, north of Maple Street.

Eli Barnum Building on lower Church Street. The Naugatuck Post Office was located in this building after the Hotchkiss Building (also called Post Office Block) on Water Street was demolished. It remained here until the post office on Church Street near Cedar Street was built in 1915.

Town hall on Church Street at Maple Street. This was an impressive structure of brick with granite trim designed by L.B. Valk of New York and dedicated on July 24, 1882. It was demolished by the Stamford Wrecking Company in April–May 1964. It once contained the town clock designed by Seth Thomas, which featured glass dials and was illuminated by the gas plant in the building.

Naugatuck Electric Light Co. on Water Street. The Electric Light Co. was organized in October 1886 with a capital of $15,000. It provided DC and AC power to the downtown area.

Interior of the Naugatuck Electric Light Co. This image shows the business as it appeared about 1895.

Town Farm on Rubber Avenue, *c.* 1900. This establishment provided food and shelter for indigent people before modern welfare programs.

Second Barnum Building, *c.* 1895. This building (on the left) housed several retail stores.

New fire house. In 1891, the Naugatuck Fire House was built on Water Street. Fire personnel began to occupy the new building in March 1892. This followed the long service of a private fire department which had protected the town since 1883.

Tolles Block on Church Street at Park Place. This building was built in 1892 as a furniture store and undertaking establishment. It was eventually destroyed by fire. Murphy's store later occupied this site.

Naugatuck National Bank, designed by McKim, Mead and White. For a while this building, completed in 1893, served both the Naugatuck National Bank and the Savings Bank. Later it was modified by Miss Gertrude Whittemore to serve as the Children's Library. It was demolished when the present town hall was built.

Whittemore Memorial Library, built in 1894. The library was constructed as a memorial to J.H. Whittemore's son, who died at age fifteen in 1887. McKim, Mead and White designed this superb classical building with a beautiful rotunda.

East side of Water Street looking south from Maple Street, 1890. The Post Office Block is beyond the Odd Fellows Building.

New John M. Page & Co. building on Church Street, c. 1895. This building was built after the planned demolition of the company's former Water Street location.

Hopson Block. In this image, the block looks as it did when it was originally built in 1896. Later, much of the fancy decorative masonry was removed to reduce masonry maintenance.

Webster Block at North Main, Oak, and Maple Street, built *c.* 1900. This block was occupied by Pierpont's Jewelry Store at the corner. The Telephone Company was on the second floor, with an entrance on Oak Street. Telephone service came to Naugatuck in 1879.

New firehouse on Maple Street, built in 1909. The new station replaced the wooden one on Water Street. The facade has since been altered.

Thomas Neary Building at Church and Maple Streets. This edifice was completed about 1909 and provided excellent facilities for several stores and businesses. Mr. Neary, who had died, formerly ran his business in the building behind it on Maple Street.

Naugatuck Savings Bank. Next to the library, this imposing structure was built in 1910 and was designed by Crowe, Lewis and Wickenhoefer of New York.

Union City Hose Company. Built on Bridge Street about 1913, this company provided fire protection for Union City. In 1918, it was temporarily used as a hospital for victims of the influenza epidemic.

Naugatuck Post Office, built in 1915. The post office was designed by James A. Wetmore, a government architect who worked for the U.S. Post Office Department.

Naugatuck YMCA. This building was designed by Jallade, Lindsay & Warren in 1922.

Naugatuck Water Company on Meadow Street. This was formerly the George A. Lewis carriage house and stable, built about 1890. It once housed a much-admired team of horses.

Naugatuck National Bank Building on Church Street, completed in 1930. A beautiful and substantial structure, this building now houses the Bank of Boston Connecticut. The interior is commodious and finely finished.

Four

Interesting Homes

As industrialists, successful merchants, and other people prospered, their improved economic circumstances often gave them a desire for larger and more impressive houses that provided increased comfort and convenience. Domestic architecture gradually shifted from simple eighteenth-century dwellings to the many styles popular at different periods during the nineteenth century. Greek Revival, Gothic, Queen Anne, and Colonial Revival were but a few of the fashions that influenced home design. The photographs here illustrate some of the styles as carried out in Naugatuck. As with fashion, in many cases what one generation thought to be the ultimate in style, the next looked on with disfavor, seeking something quite different. The train, trolley car, and automobile all played a part in changing neighborhoods. The earliest pretentious houses in Naugatuck were on North Main Street, but later the prosperous built fine homes on Church Street. Gradually more residences were built away from the center and people found smaller houses more practical than large ones requiring servants.

Joseph Lewis House on Lewis Street. Built shortly after 1730, this is probably the oldest house still standing in Naugatuck. Originally it was a small house suited to a man whose trade was weaving. He was quite successful and by 1734 he became the richest man in Judd's Meadow, owning over 700 acres of land. Through the years the house was enlarged as he prospered.

Lewis House. Joseph Lewis deeded this home, completed in 1735, and 60 acres to his son John in 1736. The house survived remarkably well for years with many fine interior details still as originally designed. This is considered the second oldest house in town.

Porter House. Built by David and his son, Thomas Porter, about 1752, this home stands near the Litchfield Turnpike. In the early days, it was a favorite stopping place for travelers. During the Revolutionary War, some of Washington's men stayed here, though not Washington himself. It is still standing and has for years been a private residence. Externally it has retained many of its original characteristics.

Jared Byington House. This abode is on the east side of town at the corner of Hill and May Streets. In 1790, Mr. Byington was making nails using a nail-cutting machine and a heading device. He obtained the second U.S. patent in Connecticut. Though the house still stands, it is so altered as to be almost unrecognizable. Mr. Byington also had a blacksmith shop and a large farm.

Beebe House on Aetna Street, built in the late 1700s. Rubber overshoes were first vulcanized in a Dutch oven when Mr. C. Beebe lived here.

Jobamah Gunn House. This was the oldest house standing in Millville until recent times, and was of the Connecticut central-hall type. It had some well-designed woodwork and mantels characteristic of the period.

Home of Amasa Goodyear and his son, Charles Goodyear. This house served the Goodyears when they came to Salem Bridge about 1805. It stood in Union City, west of Main Street near the river, until the updating of roads resulted in its removal.

Sutton Place, built on Gunn Hill (now Field Street). About 1860, this was the farmhouse of Owen Sweeney. For many years, it was owned by Joseph Frick. It is still standing and is used as a residence.

Home of Eben Tuttle. Tuttle was the inventor of the goose-neck hoe and owner of the hoe shop on Rubber Avenue, along with various other industrial operations. This Gothic-style house was the ultimate in fashion in the 1840s when Mr. Tuttle had it built on Main Street at Bridge Street. In spite of a fire, it survived until Route 8 was modernized.

B.M. Hotchkiss House on High Street, built in the 1850s. Shown here after two towers had been added, it is still standing but has been further altered.

Spencer House on Church Street. It was in its original form when Ellen and Julia Spencer were growing up, but it changed a great deal after this photograph was taken in the 1860s. John H. Whittemore came to Naugatuck and married Julia Spencer. He later had the house modernized by adding verandas and plate-glass windows. The house was eventually moved down Church Street across from the St. Francis Church and sold to Patrick Brennan, thereby making way for the large J.H. Whittemore mansion.

Robert Smith House on Hillside Avenue. This home stood on the site of the former high school (now Hillside School) until about 1902. Mr. Frederick Schaffer acquired the house and lived there until Mr. Whittemore purchased the property for a new high school. The house was moved down and across the street to become 18 Hillside Avenue. Later Mr. Schaffer moved to 56 Rockwell Avenue.

B.B. Tuttle House. For many years, domestic architecture showed little change in America, but by the 1870s new fashions were appearing. One of these was the so-called Queen Anne style, much popularized by New York architect H. Hudson Holly and his 1878 book, *Modern Dwellings*. The B.B. Tuttle House, designed by Robert W. Hill of Waterbury (before school department alterations), was one of the best examples of this high style in the United States. It was completed in 1881.

Residence of W.T. Rodenbach on Terrace Avenue. This was a Queen Anne house executed in wood instead of masonry, but retaining the high ridges and fancy chimneys characteristic of the style.

Homer Twitchell House. Twitchell, a prominent Naugatuck manufacturer making safety pins and umbrella hardware, among other things, came to Naugatuck from Oxford about 1850. He served in local public offices as well as the state legislature, as did his son after him. Homer's prosperity allowed him to build this large house on North Main Street which still exists but is much altered.

John Howard Whittemore House on Church Street. For many years, this was the most prominent house in Naugatuck. Designed in the 1880s by McKim, Mead and White, America's leading architects of the time, it contained over thirty rooms with outstanding detail and exhibited the transition from Queen Anne to Colonial Revival. It once housed a remarkable collection of fine art, antiques, books, silver, rugs, and oriental art objects, but these were dispersed at a sale in 1941.

Andrew summer home, with its multi-story tower and many windows. In clear weather, Long Island Sound could be seen from the southern panes. Destroyed by fire in 1925, the home was later rebuilt, but without the tower.

Residence of L.C. Warner on Church Street. This home was constructed when no large house seemed complete without a tower. It later became the home of Harris Whittemore Jr. and was extensively reconstructed beyond recognition to change it to a "colonial" style.

Harris Whittemore Sr. House. This shingle-style home was erected south of the "Anchorage" (home of J.H. Whittemore). The shingles were made in Middlebury and were about 1 inch thick. There were window sashes that went up into the walls. A canvas-covered ceiling that was covered with antiqued gold leaf, handsome eighteenth-century style mantels, and other remarkable features gave this house its distinctive character. At one time, this abode had been home to a most unusual collection of French Impressionist paintings. It has now been demolished.

Howard B. Tuttle House. Long a landmark on lower Millville Avenue, this was a large home with classical details. Its design was a late nineteenth-century example of the tendency to get away from ornate styling and to utilize simpler lines, employing things like Ionic pilasters.

John Vanasse House on May Street. This bungalow was built in 1919 using a Sears, Roebuck plan and material. Labor, brick, cement, and plaster cost extra and were obtained locally. The bungalow was a popular style house at that time. Sears, Roebuck furnished plans and materials for many styles of houses at the time this was built.

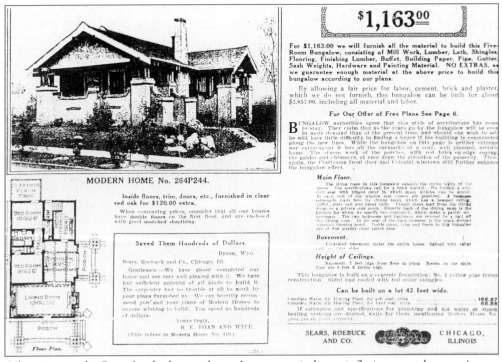

Advertisement by Sears for the house above. It seems to indicate inflation over the years!

Five

Views around Town

The Naugatuck River divides the town into two portions, each of which has a fairly level but narrow section along the river, with hills rising from it on each side. This was an attractive valley until industry somewhat filled it with factories and factory housing. Later, attempts were made to greatly improve the appearance of the town by landscaping the Green, designing the horseshoe north of Salem School, and building the granite stairs to the high school of 1904.

The photographs in this chapter illustrate some of the park areas but also show familiar street scenes and the area as viewed from various angles. With the loss of some buildings along Church Street the area has changed, but many landmarks do remain.

Looking west from the east side of town in 1865. This view shows the town center with important buildings starting at left: St. Michael's Church, the Methodist church, the Union District School on the Green, the Congregational church, the Goodyear buildings on Maple Street, and the houses along Church and Water Streets. The St. Francis Church is to the right of center. An important cabinet-making shop can be seen at the lower center. At the time of this picture, Naugatuck's population was 2,700.

View looking east from Recreation Field around 1900.

Old Maple Street bridge, as seen from Water Street below Maple Street. The board fences on either side of roadway on the bridge were so the horses could not see the river and be frightened by its flow.

View from the east side of the river, c. 1885. The B.B. Tuttle house and the building (far right) that had served as the Beecher Inn can be seen in this photograph.

Aerial photograph, c. 1940. Looking east one can see the old town hall of 1882 and many of

the U.S. Rubber Company buildings.

View of the bridge built in 1882 by the Berlin Iron Works. Nichol's Block can be seen on the left.

Looking up Church Street, c. 1890. This view shows: (left) St. Michael's Church, the Civil War monument, and the Congregational church; (right) the town hall with its prominent clock tower, and the Methodist church after it was moved from Water Street.

Looking south toward the west side of Water Street from Maple Street, about 1890.

Looking down Maple Street from Church Street, c. 1890. Freedman's clothing store occupied the old Methodist church by this time. The cylindrical horse watering trough was a prominent feature at the junction of Church and Maple Streets.

Looking northeast about 1885. St. Michael's Church, with its horse sheds, and the Union District School are visible. This view was taken after the old St. Michael's Church had been purchased by the town and moved to the north side of the school to provide additional classroom space for an expanding population. The Congregational church occupies a prominent position, and north of it is its parsonage, later moved to Meadow Street.

Complex of rubber shop buildings from Maple Street extending south to Rubber Avenue. At the far right is the back of the Page building; to its left is the Tolles block of 1892, later the site of Murphy's store.

Panoramic view looking northeast about 1895. The newly completed Salem School (1894), the recently completed St. Francis Church of 1890 (far left), and the Congregational Parish House of 1888 can be seen.

CLUB HOUSE. GOLF LINKS.
NAUGATUCK. CONN.

Club house of the Naugatuck Golf Club, as it appeared early in this century. It was built in the popular shingle style of that period.

Maple Street looking north from South Main Street, about 1905. The Hodson Cafe and Block and the Commercial Hotel north of it are on the west side of Main Street.

Looking west on Maple Street across the bridge. Town hall can be seen in the distance.

Park Place. This *c.* 1920 view is from Meadow Street, showing the Tolles (Twitchell) Block in the distance and the Masonic Building.

Church Street seen from in front of town hall. Note the trees along the grass borders between the sidewalks and road. These were removed when the streets were widened as a result of increased automobile traffic. The astounding change in the appearance of Church Street took place in the 1930s.

Looking south on Meadow Street, about 1900. This was before some of the houses on the east side were removed to make room for the St. Francis convent and parking area.

Looking east on Maple Street, about 1910. Carrington (Whittemore) Block is on the left beyond town hall, and the Neary Building is on the right. The horse drinking fountain is in the center.

Alcazar moving-picture theater, 15 North Main Street, early 1920s.

South Main Street, c. 1920. This view was taken looking north from Kennedy's Corner before it was paved.

Demolition of the Post Office (Hotchkiss) Block. The block was removed to make way for the rerouting of the railroad tracks. Notice the new wooden trestle (right) carrying the tracks along the river before the embanking covered the trestle.

Looking west from the boiler-house chimney on Water Street. The horseshoe, the granite steps, and the new high school building of 1904 can be seen.

Looking west about 1910. Homes are visible along Fairview Avenue, with extensive growth around Millville Avenue. Notice the new side streets in the area.

Looking toward Fairview Avenue from the south end of the newly expanded playground at Salem School. The stone building (left) had public facilities and a storage area for playground equipment, but was demolished a few years ago because it had fallen into a state of disrepair.

Bird's-eye view, c. 1950. One can see many of the downtown buildings around the Green.

World War II Memorial Day parade on Maple Street, c. 1948. This shot was taken in front of the Goodyear India Rubber Glove office.

Six
Sports Heroes

A brief photo essay of our town prior to 1960 would not be complete without featuring a few of our numerous sports heroes. Naugatuck has for many years fostered a rich tradition in all of the major spectator sports and has been a leading contender in the Naugatuck Valley League in particular. Our athletes have been provided with outstanding facilities and fan support for local teams is well above average. Our coaches have dedicated themselves to the teaching of sound fundamentals and the community has responded overwhelmingly with its support. Many outstanding teams and individual stars have been a result of this effort. Some have advanced to the professional ranks.

A partial list of stars would include: Dick Tuckey, Dom Minicucci, Emmett Freeman, Bill Karaban, George Goodwin, Ray Foley, Adm. Ray DuBois, Ray Anderson, Bill Moody, Fran Schildgen, and Lenny King in football; Bill Stokes, Johnny Grebb, Eddie Butkus, Jack Stinson, and Dr. Gerry Labriola in basketball; James Bradshaw, Dick Tuckey, Spec Shea, and Gene Czaplicki in baseball; Al Ratkiewich, Charley White, Regina Sullivan, Lois Ratkiewich, Jim McNamee, the Pranulis brothers, John Gabrielson, and Wayne Pawlowski in swimming; Billy Burke with his brothers Pete and Eddie, Jack Strew, Richie Gesseck, and Donna Leary in golf; Frankie Edmonds in track and field (in addition to football, basketball, and baseball); and Chick Lawson in wrestling.

Peter J. Foley. Foley's coaching career spanned three decades and produced championship teams in three major sports. His football teams won six state championships. Five of his basketball teams won state titles and even won the New England title in 1942. The 1928 and 1929 basketball teams won the Eastern States title and advanced to the nationals in Chicago. Foley was an original Naugatuck Hall of Famer and was honored with a Gold Key award by the Connecticut Sportswriters Alliance.

Original Naugatuck High School gymnasium. This facility occupied the entire center section of the first two floors of the old high school until a fire completely gutted the interior in 1962. A running track occupied the second-floor balcony, while a basketball court took up almost the entire first floor. Following the fire, the interior was redesigned into classrooms and eventually became Hillside Middle School when the new high school was built.

Gymnasium High School, Naugatuck, Conn.

Alex Gimbo Sullivan. As an outstanding swimmer and coach, Alex accumulated over two hundred trophies, plaques, and medals while also winning twelve area cross-harbor swims. He was a member of two YMCA state championship teams and placed third in a national AAU event. He was Naugatuck's first swim coach, and fostered two college all-americans—Albie Ratkiewich (Yale) and Charley White (Ohio State). He was an initial hall of famer and received the Exchange Club's gold medal for outstanding community service.

Billy Burke (William Burkowski). Burke is considered to be Naugatuck's greatest golfer. In his first Connecticut state tournament he lost on the 36th hole of the final round. In 1931 he won the PGA US Open title after 144 holes, the longest match in Open history. He played on two Ryder Cup teams and is a member of the Naugatuck Hall of Fame as well as the National PGA Hall of Fame and the Connecticut Golf Hall of Fame.

79

Fritz Klambt. Naugatuck's legendary YMCA physical athletic director was instrumental in organizing many youth programs as an outstanding gymnast and instructor. He created the Leader Corps, which entertained at the "Y" for years, and his physical fitness programs helped to develop many Naugatuck athletes.

James Farrar. A great swimmer and coach, Farrar competed for ten years in area cross-harbor swims, always finishing in the top five. He coached several "Y" junior teams to state championships, and led Sacred Heart High to nine state and two New England titles in his tenure as head coach. Coach Farrar also led Naugy High to more than one hundred wins. He was inducted into Naugatuck's Hall of Fame in 1974.

Frank "Spec" Shea. Following his dream of becoming a New York Yankee, Shea eventually worked his way, after a stint in World War II, into the Oakland Triple-A franchise. He was called up to the Yankees in 1947, where he won the all-star game, finished the season with a 15–5 record, and started three World Series games—all won by the Yankees. He also was named Rookie of the Year. He received the Connecticut Sportswriters Gold Key and was later inducted into Naugatuck's Hall of Fame.

Raymond Legenza. Raymond's football teams won ninety games and went undefeated through two seasons while receiving five CIAC Awards of Merit. His NHS baseball teams won 80 percent of their games in twenty-four years, including thirteen NVL and four state titles, while qualifying for post-season play nineteen times. The 1970–72 teams gained national recognition for winning sixty-four consecutive games—a modern record. He is in the Connecticut High School Coaches Hall of Fame, is a local hall of famer, and has been awarded a Connecticut Sportswriters Gold Key.

Naugatuck High School basketball team, 1899. This team existed before high school sports were organized. They are shown here in the old Gem Opera House that was located within the old town hall.

Naugatuck High School football team, 1903. The following members have been identified: Att. J. Sweeney (second row, fourth from left), Ed Ahern (third row, fourth from left), and former high school principal C.P. Slade (last on the right).

Naugatuck High School baseball team, 1905. The players are, from left to right: (front row) M. Herman and P. Clifford; (middle row) unidentified, F. Zwick, R. French, H. Blumenauer, and J. O'Donnell; (back row) E. Ahern, unidentified, C. Slade, A. Wiley, J. Leary, and unidentified.

Naugatuck High School basketball team, champions in 1921–22. From left to right are: (front row) W. Harvey, E. Freeman, Capt. S. Andrew, G. Foley, A. Cattanoch; (back row) Coach P. Foley, R. Foley, G. Shay, W. Linskey, D. Hoadley, and Manager J. Monahan.

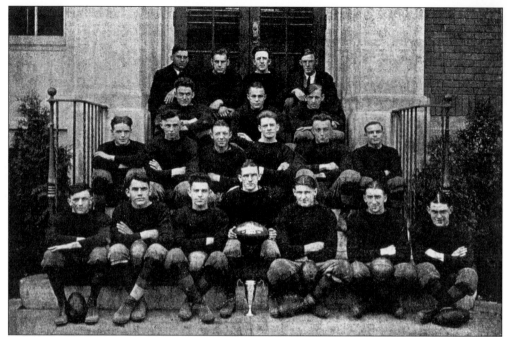

Naugatuck High School All-Naugatuck football champions, 1923. From left to right are: (front row) L. Carroll, A. Borgnis, H. Churchill, E. Carroll, H. Schwartz, T. Scanlon, and L. Lengyel; (second row) H. Carter, F. Talbot, T. St. John, A. Sullivan, A. Schmitz, and J. Shanley; (third row) P. Coffey, J. Vest, and B. Stinson; (back row) C. Walsh, W. Woermer, P. Fox, and G. Foley.

Naugatuck High School state football champions in 1928. From left to right are: (front row) L. Triano, S. Stieski, J. Biernacki, Capt. E. Butkus, W. Daly, J. Rozini, and H. Sodloski; (second row) H. "Red" Stapleton, N. Nauges, J. Lengyel, J. Gibbud, G. Woolson, A. Anderson, A. Samborski, and E. Garrick; (third row) G. Goodwin, T. Curtin, F. Hermonat, R. Goggin, W. Scully, Bob Scally, P. Beardsley, and A.Wooster; (fourth row) G. Hobbs, A. Evans, J. Balinsky, G. Kennedy, F. Reilly, J. White, E. Carroll, and Rev. F. Squires; (back row) Coach P. Foley and Mgr. W. Davis.

Naugatuck High School womens championship basketball team of 1932. The players are, from left to right: (front row) A. Erickson (player manager), E. Duff, B. Sims, Capt. S. Pocoski, H. Bergen, R. Linskey, and E. Barnum; (back row) I. Schwartz, Coach E. Kenney, and M. Chmielewski.

Naugatuck High School championship basketball team of 1927–28—on to Chicago! This team won the Eastern States Championships at the University of Pennsylvania. From left to right are: (front row) J.White, E. Carroll, Capt. B. Stokes, E. Butkus, and J. Grebauskas; (second row) J. Patterson, J. Rozint, R. Goggin, and J. Murphy; (third row) unidentified, N. Johnson, and W. Karaban; (back row) Coach P.J. Foley and Mgr. J. Reynolds. Both the 1927–28 and 1928–29 teams won at Philadelphia and went to Chicago. The 1930 and 1931 teams both won the Connecticut State Championships.

Naugatuck High School state football champions of 1932. Coach Peter J. Foley claimed this to be the greatest football team he ever coached. They even played and won against college football teams. From left to right are: (front row) T. Scally, L. Kechkes, E. Balinsky, E. Galeski, A. Nauges, D. Kirk, E. Mooney, D. Cowan, D. Minicucci, W. Moody, and R. Dubois; (back row) F. Marinello, J. Dillon, D. Tuckey, E. McDonough, W. St. John, M. Jankowski, P. Einik, W. Crosby, and E. Enamait.

Naugatuck High School 1939–40 basketball team (state and New England runner-ups). From left to right are: (front row) J. Dunn, V. Cuddy, Capt. E. Czaplicki, R. Loman, and J. Farrar; (back row) E. O'Connor, an unidentified Mgr., H. Swiderski, E. Duffy, T. Rowley, B. McDermott, Mgr. L. Noyes, and O. Garlinski.

Naugatuck High School state and New England basketball champions, 1942. From left to right are: (front row) D. Thurston, E. Mariano, B. Reilly, L. Dunn, and F. Furs; (back row) M. Kloc, Mgr. J. Reilly, J. Kissane, F. Ruccio, C. Fogarty, F. Ryan, C. Matuszewski, and D. Zehnder.

Naugatuck American Legion Post #17, state champions, 1946. This was the first team and the first state championship for the Junior League program. Representing the state in the Eastern Regionals in Glens Falls, New York were, from left to right: (front row) Coach D. Cowan, J. Healy, B. Stauffer, F. San Angelo, V. Healy, C. Boettger, B. Markovic, G. Schuster, and Business Mgr. E. Nolde; (back row) R. Currier (bat boy), F. Sokoloski, C. Uszakiewicz, B. Natowich, E. Furtado, B. Mascola, B. Stinson, and J. Curtin.

Naugatuck High School 1955 baseball team, NVL and Connecticut state champions. From left to right are: (front row) R. Stinson, J. Karbowicz, D. Doiron, R. Crelan, R. Mallane, R. Marinko, and A. Zonas; (second row) J. Casper, B. Carey, G. Zmyzemski. F .Henriques, C. Doyle, and C. Cilyo; (third row) B. Lawlor, T. Daley, M. Daly, R. Rossi, J. Marinello, and T. McDermott; (fourth row) Coach R. Legenza, T. Kopp, J. Crotty, Mgr. J. Scullin, and Assistant Coach E. Mariano.

Peter J. Foley Little League Stadium, Scott Street, built in 1948–49. This was the first little league stadium in New England. Among its board of directors in Naugatuck was Ralph Stotz, brother of Carl Stotz, the founder of the National Little League Program in Williamsport, Pennsylvania. The U.S. Rubber Co. was very instrumental in financially supporting this construction.

Seven
Industrial Beginnings

From an early date, industry played a prominent part in town development, starting out with the fulling mill on Fulling Mill Brook in the early eighteenth century and progressing to the larger factories and mills. Button manufacturing was important through much of the nineteenth century. Early on, water provided the power, but with the coming of the railroads in 1848, coal could be transported with ease and steam power became the dominant force in providing power to run machinery.

In the period between 1820 and 1850, Salem Bridge clocks were famous for their unique qualities. First manufactured here on Water Street in the 1820s by the Clark brothers from Plymouth, the business was carried on later by the Ward, Spencer, and Hotchkiss families, among others, until much cheaper clocks from Plymouth and Bristol made it impossible to compete.

Eventually, a wide diversity of industries evolved, many continuing for years until labor costs, high taxes, and other factors drove much business out of Connecticut. A few of the factories illustrated here still exist, but many have ceased operations. This situation exists in much of New England—where formerly there were thriving industrial communities, now much of the industry is gone. One wonders what the future holds for towns where the sources of their prosperity no longer exist.

Tuttle Hoe Shop on Rubber Avenue, *c.* 1870. This is where the famous shock-absorbing Tuttle hoe was made in large quantities, as well as rakes and other farm implements.

Connecticut Cutlery Company. Knives and shears were manufactured here, and the company was known for some time as the "shear shop." After the Union City Thimble Company burned in 1892, the owners bought this building and continued their production of steel thimbles here until about 1896.

E.F. Smith Button Company as it appeared about 1866. The button company was located on the north side of Prospect Street, across from the Smith homestead. These buildings burned in 1902 but the business continued in another building until 1912, when that building burned as well.

New England Button Company, c. 1885.

Dunham Hosiery Company plant on Rubber Avenue at the foot of Church Street. This was the site of a local woolen mill that produced satinet in the period between 1850 and 1876. After that time it was sold to Dunham interests in Hartford, which operated it as a mill, making knit goods. Later it became the T.F. Butterfield Company, which molded bakelite products.

Homer Twitchell & Son buildings at the foot of Prospect Street. Umbrella hardware was manufactured here. This is the complex as it appeared about 1890. It had been a machine shop earlier, and later was the Naugatuck Manufacturing Company until the flood of 1955 destroyed the buildings and ended the manufacture of copper floats for valves.

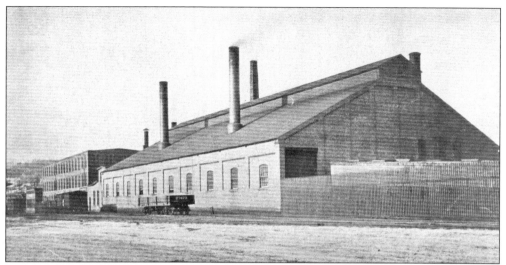

Naugatuck Malleable Iron Company on Bridge Street, *c.* 1895. Founded by B.B. Tuttle and J.H. Whittemore in 1858, it became one of the leading producers of malleable iron in America.

White & Wells Box Shop in Naugatuck. This shop was a branch of the Waterbury firm that manufactured large quantities of paper and cardboard boxes for industry.

Perry Press, c. 1923. This firm operated as a printer and binder for many years at 168 City Hill Street. The building was later destroyed by fire.

John M. Russell Manufacturing Company in the Millville section of town. This company was a small but successful manufacturer of sash and plumbers chains. Cleverly designed automatic machines stamped out links in bronze and brass and formed them into chain. Shown here in the 1940s, the company is now defunct. The building was demolished recently.

Peter Paul, Inc. This world-famous candy manufacturer started as a small candy kitchen operation, and through vision and sound management, the company experienced remarkable growth. It is now a part of the Hershey chocolate enterprise.

Risdon Manufacturing Company. This business started out as the Risdon Tool Company. About 1910 it decided to move to Naugatuck from Waterbury and to start producing small items like safety pins, eventually going heavily into deep drawing with great success. It is well known for its metal specialty work.

View of the Naugatuck Glass Company, a Bridge Street landmark for many years. This firm was begun on Elm Street by W.S. Witherwax, who had been with the Waterbury Clock Company. In 1916, the supply of clock glass from Europe was cut off. This necessitated processing glass in the United States, and so Mr. Witherwax established this business.

Last remnant of the Eastern Company (formerly the Eastern Malleable Iron Company). The Eastern Company once had plants in several cities in the United States. Naugatuck was the company's home office for many years, and there was a plant in town covering about 9 or 10 acres with numerous foundry operations. Though highly successful for over a hundred years, it is an example of what has happened to much manufacturing in the United States in recent decades.

96

Eight
The Workplace

As Naugatuck grew in population, demand for goods increased, resulting in growing commercial activity, especially in retail trade. Included here are eighteen photographs showing many retail establishments that offered everything from food to art goods. In addition to retail stores there are pictures of some of the other commercial ventures that filled many needs, such as banking, fuel, and ice. The supermarket concept has largely eliminated the small shopkeeper, often creating an impersonal relationship where there used to be a much greater intimacy between proprietor and customer.

Interior view of the John M. Page Co. Mr. Page, Mr. Buck, and several clerks in the household goods department on the ground floor pose with a variety of crockery, china, kerosene lamps, and chandeliers. Page's also sold material such as sheet metal, bar stock, etc. for industrial use.

Furniture department. This display is made up of carpet sweepers, rather flimsy plant stands, easels for large framed pictures, and a wide choice of wicker rockers (which were quite popular in the 1890s).

Sweeney's Art Store. An early tenant of the Neary Building, Sweeney's carried a wide range of framed and unframed pictures and other popular art objects. It had some of the latest appurtenances such as a large fancy cash register and combination gas and electric light fixtures. This popular store was located here for many years.

Meat market on Main Street at turn of the century. Note the electric lights and fans and many hooks for hanging meat. The store also had the convenience of a telephone. The electric wiring is of the knob and tube type used in the early days of electrical distribution.

Interior of the new bank building just north of the town hall. Mr. Dayton of the Savings Bank is facing the camera and is looking toward the Savings Bank window. At the time this photograph was taken, the building was used by both the National Bank and the Savings Bank. In 1910 the latter built its own building north of the library.

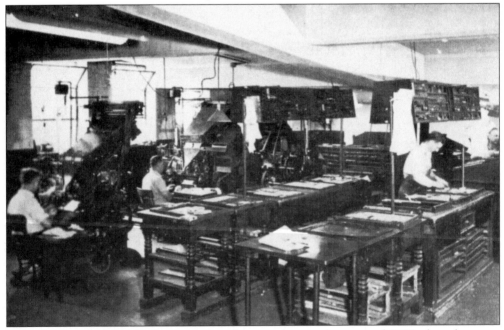

Offices of the *Naugatuck Daily News*. This photograph was taken around 1935 when the paper was located at 9–11 North Main Street.

Dye room at the Dunham Mills, *c.* 1900.

Dr. Gorton's waiting room at his dental parlors in Water Street. The stove in the doorway provided heat for both the waiting room and the operating room.

View of what was considered a well-equipped dental establishment. Notice the plush-covered furniture and the tablecloths reaching to the carpet—not what would be considered hygienic today!

Risdon Manufacturing Company's lathe department. The company had up-to-date fluorescent lighting installed, but the machines, shown here being set up for production operations, were still run by overhead shafting. Later machinery had integral motors, which were far safer for operators.

Taylor's Market on Water Street, *c.* 1915.

Buildings of the John M. Page Co., *c.* 1885. This view was taken when it was located on the west side of Water Street south of Maple Street.

E.J. Sweeney's store at 58 Water Street, *c*. 1895. Sweeney's sold window glass, picture frames, and cabinet work. It also carried on a locksmithing business.

Fremont W. Tolles furniture store at 49–51 Church Street, *c*. 1890.

Lundin Cooperative Grocery Store on Hillside Avenue, corner of Grove Street, *c.* 1895.

Members of the Pond Hill Ice Co. cutting ice on May Street, 1895.

Nichols Service Station, North Church Street, *c.* 1935.

Naugatuck Fuel Company on Church Street, *c.* 1945. This was the agency for Ford cars in Naugatuck.

Nine
Modes of
Transportation

For many years horses were the only mode of transportation, and only the fairly well-to-do could afford the space and equipment they required. In the 1700s people rarely went beyond the limits of their town.

Naugatuck was located on the Litchfield Turnpike connecting New Haven and Litchfield by stagecoach. Since it was necessary to rest or change horses after certain distances were traveled, it was customary to stop for refreshment at inns along the way. A couple of favorite stops between New Haven and Litchfield were the Collins Hotel in Straitsville, and the Beecher Inn in Salem Bridge, across the street from the tollhouse, which stood on Church Street near the dam.

In 1849 the Naugatuck Railroad was created to serve the Naugatuck River Valley towns. By 1880 the New England Railroad also passed through the northern part of town and provided transport to Danbury, Newburgh, and other destinations.

Later, trolley service was established to Waterbury and other points. With the coming of the automobile, the travel picture changed beyond anyone's wildest dreams. This change brought about better and well-marked roads.

Attempts to make airplanes in Naugatuck were interesting but the enormous capital required was not forthcoming, so these efforts did not bear lasting fruit.

Bicycling along the Naugatuck River, *c.* 1890.

Horse and buggy, *c.* 1895.

Horses and a horse-drawn wagon in front of Nichols Block on South Main Street, *c.* 1890.

Salem Spring Ice Company delivery wagon No. 1. This business was located at 50 Water Street.

Delivery wagon of A.E. Curtiss, dealer in meats at 6 Church Street, *c.* 1895.

Sales and advertising wagon for Owl hooks and eyes. As the wagon moved, the owl turned.

Original Naugatuck railroad station. This station stood off Maple Street near the place where the firehouse was later built. After tracks were rerouted to follow the river, this building was moved to Hillside Avenue above Bradbury Street for use as an office, but it was never used as such and was demolished around 1930.

Train stopped at the old station. The J.M. Page building is visible in the background.

Stone arch, built in 1880. This is the once well-known and superbly constructed stone arch that carried the tracks of the New England Railroad over North Church Street (now Route 63). It was wide enough for only one automobile to pass. The stones were dovetailed, and when it came time to begin demolition in 1940, it was necessary to enlist the help of a surviving workman from Sharon to point out the keystone.

The wooden trestle that connected to the stone arch, built in 1880. This trestle was later completely covered by embanking it. The lower arch for water passage still stands near Hop Brook Dam.

The Webster Block at Main, Maple, and Oak Streets. The second floor, with its stairs and entrance on Oak Street, contained the Naugatuck Telephone Exchange. The building was demolished for Route 8 improvements. The trolley tracks occupied the road center.

A 1924 Model-T Ford. This was the car that people of modest means could afford and the product that changed the course of life in America.

113

Early automobile, complete with acetylene head lamps, *c.* 1910.

Pond Hill Ice Company's Mack truck with chain drive, *c.* 1910.

L.V. Matson & Son's Packard lumber truck, *c.* 1920.

Combination hearse and ambulance of Walter H. Twitchell, furniture dealer and undertaker in Tolles Block, 132–136 Church Street, 1919.

Burke's Dairy Dodge truck, *c.* 1926.

Fleet of the Naugatuck Chemical Company, 1928.

Wilson F. Clark fleet of trucks, *c.* 1938.

Clark Oil Truck, *c.* 1941.

Local airplane by John Nixon, 1921.

Streamlined aircraft by Cairns Aircraft, *c*. 1930.

Ten

The U.S. Rubber Company

In the Naugatuck Valley, this town was often called the "rubber town." Charles Goodyear's father had moved to Naugatuck from New Haven when Charles was about five years old. This was to have a major influence on the development of Naugatuck. Some years later, Charles became fascinated with crude rubber and realized it might have possible uses. The story of accidental vulcanization on a laboratory stove is well known. It took a while to get the necessary financial backing to carry on experiments to perfect this process. By 1843, Goodyear was able to undertake the manufacture of rubber shoes and out of this developed an industry that employed thousands of people here. It is not possible in this space to give the details of this complex story. Goodyear was highly inventive and obtained many patents, but was a poor business man. By his death in 1860 he had lost control of the business, which was carried on by others. The pictures used here show various aspects of the Goodyear (later the U.S. Rubber) business with several departments and some of the personnel.

Tennis Mill.

Office and sales room of the Goodyear Metallic Rubber Shoe Co.

Phoenix Shop on Maple Street, with the engine house at the corner of Water Street, c. 1895. In the background, one can see the town hall clock tower, and the tower of the old Congregational church to its right on the Green. Over the intersection is an early electric arc street light.

Early view of Maple and Water Streets with the Maple Street wooden bridge. When the dam on the river was built in 1824 it was to provide water power for Silas Grilley's button shop (right) on Water Street. This was soon sold to Sylvester and Heman Clark, who manufactured their highly regarded Salem Bridge clocks here.

Aerial view of the footware complex.

Naugatuck Chemical buildings, *c.* 1910.

Close-up of some of the older Naugatuck Chemical buildings.

Synthetic Plant buildings, *c.* 1950.

Funeral for a dignitary on Maple Street, about 1900.

Old Glove Company No.1 cutting room, *c.* 1910.

Interior of the G.M.R. Co. boot room, 1910.

Interior of boot-making department, *c*. 1900.

Goodyear M.R.S. Co. office and staff on Rubber Avenue.

GIR Glove Co. personnel in front of the central office (Building 25), 1920.

Warehouse on Rubber Avenue. Parts of this complex had once been the Spencer and Hotchkiss (later the Spencer and Wooster) Clock Company.

Acknowledgments

Much appreciation is extended to the following:

Photo Committee members:
Dana Blackwell
Verna Blackwell
Howard Burke, chairman
Sandra Clark
David Ebersole
William Ford
Robert Stauffer

Private collectors and others:
D. Almquist, J. Anderson, V. Anderson, B. Broaderick,
M. Burke, A. Clark, R. Corso, M. Nichols, K. Nixon,
S. Pocoski, H. Scally, A. Simons, and J. Vanasse